ALSO BY DON RICKLES

Rickles' Book

Rickles' Letters

DON RICKLES

with David Ritz

SIMON & SCHUSTER
New York   London   Toronto   Sydney

Simon & Schuster
1230 Avenue of the Americas
New York, NY 10020

Copyright © 2008 by Wynnefield Productions, Inc.

First Simon & Schuster hardcover edition November 2008

For information about special discounts for bulk purchases,
please contact Simon & Schuster Special Sales at
1-800-456-6798 or business@simonandschuster.com.

Designed by Ruth Lee-Mui

808.8693
RIC

Manufactured in the United States of America

10 9 8 7 6 5 4 3 2 1

Library of Congress Cataloging-in-Publication Data
Rickles, Don.
 Rickles' letters / Don Rickles with David Ritz.
    p. cm.
1. Letters—Humor. I. Ritz, David. II. Title.
  PN6231.L44R53 2008
  808.869'3—dc22   2008036272

ISBN-13: 978-1-4165-9663-9
ISBN-10:   1-4165-9663-1

For my Barbara.
You made it happen.

...and David and I thank you.

Contents

From the desk of Don Rickles

Hi gang,

Just when I was ready to tear up my high school library card, here I am trying to write a new book.

Unlike my first one, *Rickles' Book*, this one isn't fact. On the other hand, I wouldn't exactly call it fiction. Truth is, I don't know what to call it. So I'm calling it *Rickles' Letters*. Okay, so I haven't mailed any of 'em—go tell it to the FBI.

They're just crazy letters that let me express myself. After all, I'm an artist.

Besides, I'm in my eighties, so what can they do to me? Take away my milk and cookies?

What else do I have to do except write letters? How many Indian casinos can you play in one year? How many Dodgers games can one man watch?

I gotta entertain myself and, in the process, I hope to entertain you. Example: I enjoy writing kidnap letters to myself, then letting the cops figure out who's missing.

I want to reach out and write to my close

RICKLES'
LETTERS
1

 *From the desk of Don Rickles*

friends—as in the ones who send me a card every New Year's to see if I'm still alive. I also want to reach people who aren't so crazy about me—as in the ones who've seen my act and didn't bother to applaud.

I want to get more involved in American history. Like, "Dear Mrs. Lincoln, Sorry the show at Ford's Theatre didn't go well last night. But could you get me a couple of aisle seats for the Saturday matinee?"

I want to write to a lot of the stars I've known over the years, so they won't forget how I contributed to their success, and ask them to leave me something before they die—like their estates.

One last thing: None of these letters were written on a computer. I've been writing letters since before they put erasers on pencils—and that's still good enough for me.

I'm grabbing my yellow pad and getting started.

So start reading. Fasten your seat belt. Rickles is writing again.

Letters to My Friends

Mr. Kirk Douglas
Beverly Hills, California

Dear Kirk,

Kirk, Kirk, Kirk.

"Mister Energy" Douglas.

What a career you've had. *The Bad and the Beautiful.*
Champion. Lust for Life. Paths of Glory. Gunfight at the
O.K. Corral. The list goes on. The movies you've made
with Burt Lancaster. You had real class, Kirk, even though
you and Burt had to fight over the billing.

You know the thing I remember about you the most
though, Kirk? When you stood on a rock on the beach
in Malibu and asked me what I thought of your great
body. That's when I realized: You thought you really *were*
Spartacus.

RICKLES'
LETTERS
5

To be honest, you just looked like a guy in a really tight bathing suit. But then you started running up and down the beach, shouting, "Follow me, men! The ships are coming!"

Kirk, that's when I thought that maybe you were starting to lose it.

But how can I forget all the great women you have made love to—from Ava Gardner to Sylvia Schwartz . . . Oh, sorry, Kirk. Sylvia was a waitress in Buffalo, the one who did the glass and water trick.

Your friend,

Don

P.S.—Does Michael really think he's taller than you?

Michael Douglas
The Douglas Compound, Bermuda

Dear Michael,

Everyone in LA wishes you would come back—there hasn't been a good cop show in years, and somebody needs to go out to the beach to tell your dad he's not Spartacus.

Sincerely,

RICKLES'
LETTERS
7

Mr. Potato Head
Pixar Animation Studios
Burbank, California

Dear Mr. P.H.,

What is it with you? You really think you're something special?

I'll give you special.

Look in the mirror—you're a half-baked spud! Without my voice, you're through! Washed up and back in the ground in Idaho!

Let me tell you something: I was doing *Toy Story* when you were still trying to upstage bacon and sour cream. You really steam me, Mister, thinking you're bigger than Rickles. Remember, one phone call to the Boys and you're buried at the bottom of the salad bar. Either that, or somebody

cuts your cords during the Macy's parade and you end up in some deli on Broadway for lunch.

In closing, just keep the kids happy. Otherwise, you could end up a potato pancake with no breathing room. In the meantime, go oil your equipment: nose, hat, ears . . . you know, the works. It's almost time for the next movie and the folks at Disney are worried that your eyes are coming loose.

Yours truly,

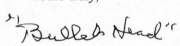
"Bullet Head"

Martin Scorsese
New York, New York

Hello Marty,

I just wanted to tell you how much I cherished the opportunity to work with a legendary master-genius such as yourself. Hang on a minute—with all these compliments, I think I'm gonna throw up.

Anyone could have played pit boss Billy Sherbert in *Casino,* but you chose me. Tell the truth, Marty—it was the short money and I had no dialogue.

What a thrill to be standing next to the great Robert De Niro, though, who kept mumbling, "You know, Marty's my best friend . . . you know, Marty's my best friend."

And I said, "Stop already, Bob! I know you guys are best friends!"

RICKLES'
LETTERS
11

Meanwhile, you paid so little that my wife and I were living in a cardboard box off Hollywood Boulevard. You didn't care—you had a Manhattan townhouse, and mumble-mouth Bobby was making a billion.

Okay, I'll see you at the movies, Marty. Waitaminute—what movies? You're doing commercials now. Well, if you need a spokesman for a "Spider" enlarger, I'm your man.

As ever,

Don

Clint Eastwood
Malpaso Productions
Burbank, California

Hey Clint,

I know you have a big following and a lot on your plate, but I'm sure you remember me. It's Rickles from *Kelly's Heroes*. A hundred years ago? Yugoslavia? Remember the laughs with Telly Savalas, Carroll O'Connor, and Donald Sutherland who, by the way, doesn't remember being there?

Look at you today: a man with a little age, but still a big star. How many guys could do a movie about Iwo Jima from the Japanese point of view? For a while there, I thought you were going to let them win!

You're big, Clint. Oh yeah, you're big: blockbuster after blockbuster, award after award, and former mayor of Carmel. Maybe it's because you owned the town.

But what about me, Clint? You could have made my day.
I know I'm just a guy from Queens who can't ride a horse,
but you still could have put me in *Unforgiven*.

Best,

DON
RICKLES
14

Jackie Collins
Bel Air, California

Dear Jackie,

You're a great novelist—telling stories of people in bed, out of bed, working on going to bed, under the bed, and in the bathroom, humming.

But Jackie, as far as these combinations go in the real world: Should a gardener really take a shot at the lady of the house while she's watering the roses? Am I to believe that a hooker can fall in love with a vice cop, run off to the porno festival in Vegas, and wind up with a multi-picture contract?

Jackie, Jackie—take it easy. Forget the books. Clean the house. Take a trip to Africa. Get to know the natives.

But then again, forget the natives. You're making $40 million a book, and I'm still writing these crazy letters to pay the rent.

Love ya,

Don,

the poor author

Hugh Hefner
The Playboy Mansion
Holmby Hills, California

Dear Hef,

We go way back. You remember the Chicago days when I first hit the Playboy clubs? It was me, Don Adams, Jimmy Caan, and Warren Beatty, all of us in heat.

At the time, I thought you were a monk. But when I came out to California, there you were: laying around the pool in nothing but your bathrobe and silk slippers, covered with broads. You must have had magnificent fire engine equipment under there.

Hef, I remember those parties like they were yesterday. A guy could really have a ball at the mansion: you'd jump into the pool, only to realize you weren't wearing a suit.

Then you found your own little corner of the grotto, your own little playmate, and learned how to deep-sea dive.

Now, after many years, I like the way you've settled down: Every night you go to bed with your bathrobe, three girlfriends, and six dogs, and watch yourselves on TV.

That's what I call retirement.

Best to the Hefner Children's Camp.

Yours truly,

Don Rickles

DON
RICKLES
18

Mr. Lou Fluke
Somewhere in Venezuela

Dear Lou,

All these years you've been one heck of a business manager and accountant. You've taken care of my finances like they were your own. So when you said you wanted to take a well-deserved vacation down to South America, I was glad to hear it.

But c'mon, that was two years ago and I haven't been able to write a check since.

Two postmen have already died trying to reach you. I sent my cousin Manny to see you, but as he swam the moat to your compound, an alligator spotted him and took an arm. I asked the Venezuelan government to investigate, but

RICKLES'
LETTERS
19

they say they're not in the alligator business. They'll only help you out if you're Jewish and need a ladies' handbag.

I miss you, Lou. Ever since you disappeared, I've had a terrible run of bad luck. I lost my house, my uncle Jack was pinned under a car while he was researching alligator diets, my aunt Rhoda went in for a kidney operation and got a brain transplant instead, and my nephew Seymour—you remember, the sensitive kid who always wanted to be a dancer—hanged himself with his ballet slippers.

I wouldn't be alarmed—I always knew you'd pay me back the $800,000 that went missing from my bank account—except I read in the paper that you just became the new secretary of the treasury down there. That made me suspicious.

Just thought you should know. By the way, I'm having an estate sale next Tuesday to pay my back taxes. In case you're interested, I have a gold-plated pistol. Ever try Russian roulette?

Sincerely,
your former client,

Don

Ed Ruscha
Santa Monica, California

Dear Ed,

I love you dearly and I'm proud to have you as my friend. The world knows you as a great modern artist. I know you as a guy who can draw a giant Hershey's bar.

I respect your work, but I can't understand how you made it. Ed, what is it with that gas station thing you drew? For seven billion?? I draw a straight line and nothing happens.

But hey, you make it work and I'm glad. Still, if you ever want a real job, come over and paint our house.

Your pal,

Michelangelo's
Cousin

RICKLES'
LETTERS
21

Suzanne Somers
Malibu, California

Dear Suzanne,

I must say, knowing you is a real delight. Why, you ask? Because your special sunny way makes you so charming on the Home Shopping Network.

Having said that, I tried the Ab Buster and my ass fell down. Then I switched to the ThighMaster, and "Spider" was crushed. It ruined my day, not to mention my night.

Next I tried your vitamin line, fully expecting Marlon Brando to emerge with a jar of candy in his mouth. It just

RICKLES'
LETTERS
23

didn't happen. Don't worry, Suzanne. I'm not giving up on your products.

I'm just not using them.

Your good friend,

Steve Lawrence & Eydie Gorme
Las Vegas, Nevada

Dear Steve and Eydie,

Hi guys—you've been beautiful friends since we all broke into show biz back in the 19th century.

Thanks so much for the flowers for my birthday—they're absolutely terrific. Except, at my age, I need to have someone smell them for me.

I know how you both love to cook, and I look forward to seeing you in Vegas at the International Meatloaf Contest.

Love,

Don

RICKLES'
LETTERS
25

Arnold Schwarzenegger, Governor
The Governor's Mansion
Sacramento, California.

Hello Governor,

First off, I honor and respect you. But I have some advice:

1. Shorten your name. What is this—stump the stars?
2. Arnold, I know you like being governor, but you were so much better as the Terminator. Between the leather jacket, the machine gun, and the one eye, you turned Halloween into Gay Pride Day.
3. Stop singing Austrian fight songs in the state capitol.
4. Lose the cigar. It's hard enough to understand you without it.

RICKLES'
LETTERS
27

5.   You gotta stop riding around town in those big black
     Hummers—funerals are starting to follow you.

Now, maybe you could help me out. My cousin
Herman's doing time in San Quentin—but all he did was
shoot a dog and beat up an old lady. Make a phone call,
Arnold. Give him a pardon. I know he'd appreciate it. Not
only that, the prison population would adore you.
     Okay, Arnold, I'll see you at the Governor's Ball. I'll be
there with my wife, and cousin Herman.

                              Best,

                              Don Bowman

                              Hugh Way

                              Patrolman

Debbie Reynolds
Las Vegas, Nevada

Dear Debbie,

Thanks for the birthday card. It brought back a lot of old memories for me—I hope it did for you too.

I guess you can't forget how I slapped you around and tore off your dress in the movie *Rat Race*. I always thought it was the highlight of your career.

I also remember when you were an adorable young woman, dancing away with Donald O'Connor and Gene Kelly. Then in the later years, I remember when your big finish was the Zsa Zsa Gabor impressions. Too bad the audience thought it was Carol Burnett.

Do you remember when we shared the stage together, Deb? I'll never forget how you always took the better

RICKLES'
LETTERS
29

dressing room. And what the hell—all these years later I finally feel safe telling you that, after the show, I'd sneak into your bathroom just to feel what it was like to use the star's toilet.

Lastly, I remember how you always loved white wine. I remember how you used to leave all the empties outside my door. You made sure there wasn't a drop left. That was your way of being Debbie.

I hear you're still performing. Maybe it's time to put the wardrobe in the closet. That way, I can borrow it.

Love ya,

Don

DON
RICKLES
30

Cher
Malibu, California

Dear Cher,

I just have to tell you that you're a fine talent, but what really makes it for me is your drop-dead wardrobe. With all the costume changes during your show, you must have a full pit crew just to oil your zippers. First you come out as Cleopatra, then you come out as Marie Antoinette, then you come out as Pocahontas . . . Why don't you just come out as Dora Schwartz and be done with it?

You also have a magnificent home in Malibu—the kind of place where you need hunting dogs just to make it from the gate to the front door. I hope you invite the wife and me up for coffee some day, just to prove that it only *looks* like a minimum-security prison.

RICKLES'
LETTERS
31

Finally, you're a smart, beautiful woman, but I also know you've had a problem settling down with Mister Right. You're in great shape, but the clock is ticking and you can't stay on the treadmill forever. Think about finding a nice guy with a truck and a dry-cleaning service.

Love,

Don

Mickey Mouse
Walt Disney Studios
Burbank, California

Dear Mickey Mouse,

    It's great how you make all the boys and girls love you at Disneyland. Whatever Walt's family is paying you, it's not enough.

    If I were you, I'd contact the well-known agent Lenny Shipman, who's sitting by the phone even as we speak. This is the same man who got Olive Oyl a four-picture deal at Paramount, and she didn't even have to kiss up to Popeye. Lenny was also responsible for getting Goofy back on his feet after he locked Cinderella in his basement for three days last July.

    Also, I got a great publicist for you. Her name is Harriet

RICKLES'
LETTERS
33

Finkel. She'll get you on *Hollywood Squares* and *American Gladiators*. She'll also make sure your balloon in the Macy's Thanksgiving Day Parade is twice as big as Mr. Potato Head's.

Just don't hold it against her that her last client was Fanny Brice.

That's about it. I consider you family, although I can't promise you'll be at the house for the High Holy Days.

Bye bye, Mickey,

Don

P.S.—Lose the gloves unless you're going into medicine.

DON
RICKLES
34

Denzel Washington
Hollywood Hills, California

Dear Denzel,

What an actor, what a star, what a career!

You're one of the finest actors on the screen today. One minute you're a Civil War soldier and the next minute you're Malcolm X. Then you're a Harlem gangster. After that, you're a school teacher.

Denzel, why don't you go home, take a nap, and figure out once and for all who you're really supposed to be.

It's a shame you never played in the NBA. I'm joking. You're great, Denzel, and I compare you to my close

personal friend, Sidney Poitier. When I'm with Sidney, by the way, he never mentions your name.

Denzel, I gotta run. Sidney's having a cocktail party. Damn shame you weren't invited.

As ever,

Bob Newhart
Beverly Hills, California

Dear Bob,

You, Ginnie, Barb, and I have traveled the world together. The tab was always split straight down the middle, even though you ordered two times as much as me, and that pissed me off.

All those cruises we took, especially when we went to Vietnam, where people always recognized you. Just because I didn't have a hit TV show didn't mean I was jealous; I just thought it would be funny to tell the North Vietnamese guide that you planned to knock him off.

Bob, you're a great guy, but I have to tell you: You're a square. When we went to Paris and dined at the Ritz, did

you have to order a salami sandwich on Wonder Bread with mayo?

How could a farmer from the Midwest and a classy guy like me from New York ever be this close? The key is the wives. Barb and Ginnie are as close as sisters. We just tag along to shine their jewelry.

You and Ginnie will always be in our hearts.

Love always,

Don

Barbra Streisand
Malibu, California

Dear Barbra,

I've known you a long time and am writing to let you know what a great fan I am instead of just waving to you at cocktail parties.

What a voice! What a talent! What a bonus that you married a great guy like Jim Brolin! I remember when my former manager, Joe Scandore, an Italian from Ocean Parkway, bought a house next to Jim's ranch. Jim thought it'd be fun to teach Joe how to ride a horse.

Now Joe's ass is in a museum.

Seriously, Barbra, I know you're into interior decoration and home expansion. But I hear the new plans for your house are so big you asked the Malibu city council to move

the ocean back ten feet, including the waves. If anybody can get it done, it's Streisand.

I also hear that you plan to adopt Marvin Hamlisch. Great idea. Now you'll have an in-house piano tuner for life. I know that when it comes to recording you're a perfectionist. But did you have to slap Marvin in front of the whole orchestra when he hit that wrong note?

We all look forward to more records, more movies, and more concerts. And at $6,000 a seat, I'm sure you, Jim, and Marvin will be set for life.

Like you're not already.

Love,

DON
RICKLES
40

David Ritz
Los Angeles, California

Dear David,

Just a note to let you know how much I've enjoyed writing *Rickles' Book* and now *Rickles' Letters* with you. Now stop calling me and telling me what a big help you've been. To hear you tell it, you're Hemingway and I'm the guy who sharpens your pencils.

David, every time you come to the house to write with me, you demand lunch. That wasn't part of the deal. To make matters worse, you always want a potato knish, which has been proven to kill anyone over forty.

That's it, David. I'm proud to have worked with

someone whose co-writing credits include Ray Charles, Marvin Gaye, B.B. King, and Smokey Robinson, but you should probably know I'm not black.

Yours for a literary future,

DON
RICKLES

LOS ANGELES, CALIFORNIA

Anne Peters, M.D.
USC Medical Center

Dear Anne,

What a blessing you are in my life! Before I met you, I thought diabetes was a horse that ran in the Kentucky Derby. Good thing I didn't put any money on him, otherwise I'd be on the critical list at Cedars-Sinai Medical Center.

Anne, I know you're a world-class endocrinologist, even though I don't know what that word means. Thank God. If it weren't for you, I'd have turned into a Hershey bar. Thank you for educating me about the dangers of diabetes and giving me a 20 percent discount on every visit.

Love, your loyal patient,

RICKLES'
LETTERS
43

DON
RICKLES
LOS ANGELES, CALIFORNIA

Eliot Weisman
Miami Beach, Florida

Dear Eliot,

Let's have a fireside chat. We all know you managed Liza Minnelli, Sammy Davis, Jr., Steve and Eydie, and Sinatra. But did you ever dream you'd manage the one guy that caught on? You've come to my shows, you've come to my home, and you've come to my parties, and you've always wanted a commission for it.

Eliot: I think it's time for me to play bigger venues. I wasn't thrilled when you had me headline at the Fallsburg bridge tournament. You keep promising the Kennedy Center Honors, and the closest I've been is the coffee shop at the Mayflower Hotel in Washington.

I'm kidding. You know I love you and it doesn't matter that you're holding me back.

Your favorite client
(when the moon is right)

Tony Oppedisano
Toluca Lake, California

Dear Tony O,

You are my loyal road manager and friend. We met years ago when you were playing mandolin and singing at a lounge in Lake Tahoe. Just when you were about to make a big move, you were thoughtful enough to give it all up to help me on the road. We've had some great laughs together: In and out of limos. In and out of airports. In and out of gas stations. In and out of immigration. In and out of security. All the while, you were carrying my bags—now that's class.

The only hitch we ever had was at the Canadian border, where customs officers questioned you about a bank robbery in San Diego. With a last name like Oppedisano, it was an

uphill battle, but after two hours of my swearing up and down that you were innocent, they finally let you go. It wasn't until we were safely in the limo on the way to the hotel that I asked, "Where'd you bury the money?"

I love you, Tony, and tell Mom Rose to send over her delicious veal piccata.

Love,

Ernest Borgnine
Beverly Hills, California

Dear Ernie,

We've shared a lot of memories over the years: Both of us serving in World War II, both of us on screen together in *The Rabbit Trap.*

At the top of the list, though, one memory sticks out. It was the time we shared the stage in *The Odd Couple.* Because you had already won an Oscar for *Marty,* I would have followed you anywhere. And after a few thousand rehearsals, you finally thought we were ready.

"Just one thing, Don," you said.

"Sure, Ernie."

"Whatever you do, stick to the script."

"Anything you say, Ernie."

Opening night. First act. Curtain goes up—I stick to my lines. The audience laughs—I stick to my lines. Curtain comes down—I stick to my lines.

Second act. Curtain goes up—I stick to my lines. Audience laughs—you get the picture.

Then a stage light blows out. Me? I stick to my lines. You, Ernie? You ad lib for two minutes straight, apologizing to the audience.

Thank God the critics said we were great.

And thanks for letting me polish your Oscar.

Fondly,

Don

DON
RICKLES
50

DON
RICKLES
LOS ANGELES, CALIFORNIA

Conrad Hermogenes
North Hollywood, California

Dear Conrad,

I'm a lucky man to have you as my personal assistant. Even though you are now an American citizen, I call you the Man from Manila.

I don't hold it against you that my two-and-a-half-year stint in the Navy, stationed in the Philippines, was a hardship. I didn't mind saving your country, but it was too damn hot while I was doing it.

Conrad, I want you to know I appreciate you. But if your entire family decides to visit the United States, there's definitely no room at my place.

With gratitude,

RICKLES'
LETTERS
51

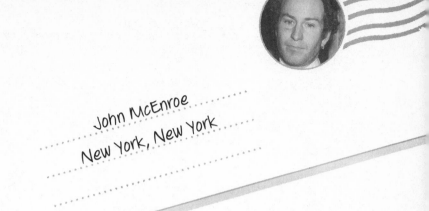

John McEnroe
New York, New York

Dear John,

What's tennis without the great McEnroe? Who could forget the day at Forest Hills when you got angry at the umpire and ate the net? Then there was the time at Wimbledon when you stopped the match to beat up the ball boy. What class! And then the highlight of your career: You won the Australian Open, lifted the trophy over your head, and threw it at your opponent's family.

Fortunately, Barbara and I got to know you and Patty on a personal basis. You were gracious enough to come to our beach house in Malibu. But when I offered you a cold beer,

instead of thanking me, did you have to throw your sneakers against the wall?

John, you're a great guy, and I only have one suggestion: Valium.

Love ya,

David Rosenthal
Simon & Schuster
New York, New York

Dear David,

You're the powerful chief of an international publishing company. Why am I talking this way? I've already got a book deal.

Writing with Ritz has been stimulating, and we didn't mind that you gave us an entire two weeks to do this new book.

Now let's talk about improving my lifestyle. Last time, you gave us a lovely book party at Elaine's, but did you have to have Elaine stand on the bar and dance the Hawaiian Hora? I also thought inviting the building inspector from the Bronx wasn't such a good idea, especially when he kept spitting out nails on my uncle Irving's pants.

Mel Tormé's cousin Phil was an interesting choice for entertainment, even though he did sing while juggling soft tomatoes.

David, forget the party this time. How about sending me and the Mrs. on a safari—because you know how Jews love to hunt.

Yours truly,
Your favorite author

DON
RICKLES
LOS ANGELES, CALIFORNIA

Joe Mele
Las Vegas, Nevada

Dear Joe,

You're a musical genius. You were one of the Four Lads.
You were Patti Page's musical director, even though you
threw Patti's doggie out the window and into traffic.

The highlight of your career, though, had to be twenty
years ago when you became my musical director. You crafted
my shows. You even became the straight man. You didn't
object when I noticed you were tone-deaf and you didn't blink
an eye when, one opening night, seven of your band members
were missing. The music was a little thin, but we got by.

You and I will always carry a tune together.

Love ya,

Chris Rock
Brooklyn, New York

Dear Chris,

Doing that joint interview with you in *Rolling Stone* gave me an idea:

You and I can be the new Crosby and Hope. I'll be Crosby; I'll wear the hat. You'll be Hope; just grab a golf club and lighten up the makeup.

They'll love us in Morocco. We'll kill 'em in Rio. And with any luck, we can work the States as long as you don't tell Bud Freeman we're not going to play his comedy club on Melrose Avenue.

What do you say, Chris? Are we going to make this work, or are you going back to busting your macaroons

RICKLES'
LETTERS
59

writing HBO specials instead of hooking up with me, the Great Legend?

Stick with me, kid, and there's a good chance we can replace Manilow at the Hilton.

See you opening night.

Your possible partner,
Love ya,

Letters to People
I Don't Know but Who
Need My Advice

Benjamin Franklin
Independence Hall
Philadelphia, Pennsylvania

Dear Benjamin Franklin,

Enough with the lightning . . . fly the kite on a sunny afternoon! My cousin Seymour had a successful candle business, and you had to go ahead and ruin it with this electricity business. Try thunder—maybe there's something in it for you.

Yours for a brighter future,

Don, the Light
merchant

RICKLES'
LETTERS
63

Dear Bonnie,

You're a lovely young girl. I know you're doing well in school. But I'm worried about you and need to give you some advice.

First off, all the Tommy Gun practice is keeping the neighbors up. They said they'd be happy to buy you a silencer if it means a good night's sleep.

Secondly, you come on awfully strong. I know young people these days like to run a little fast, but when I caught you rolling around the grease pit in your bra and panties with the local auto mechanic, I thought you were taking it too far. And the way you worked over some of our farm boys? No wonder they didn't want to go home in the off-season.

Now you're in love with this young fellow Clyde. He's a nice young man, good looking guy, and I believe him when he tells me he's got a future in banking . . . But does he have to shoot the teller just because he has bad teeth?

I sincerely hope the two of you come to your senses and settle down. I know how much Clyde loves cars—maybe the two of you could open a Toyota dealership in Newark.

Sincerely,

Don Rickles

DON
RICKLES
66

DON
RICKLES
LOS ANGELES, CALIFORNIA

Joe Torre, Manager
Los Angeles Dodgers
Dodger Stadium, Los Angeles, California

Dear Joe,

Welcome to LA.

Tommy Lasorda is thrilled about your arrival. Now you have someone to talk to in Italian. Too bad he canceled the parade for you, but when he found out he couldn't be in the lead car . . . well, we all knew you'd understand. Hey, at least you don't have to wash and wax Steinbrenner's Rolls-Royce anymore, not to mention picking up the Boss's dry cleaning.

But let's talk baseball, because I think you've got the right attitude for the Dodgers. It took nerve to tell Frank McCourt he couldn't play in the outfield. It took guts to send

RICKLES'
LETTERS
67

the pitching staff back to the Dominican Republic to work the sugarcane fields.

By the way, if you find yourself at a Hollywood party and things get a little wild, hit a few pop flies into the living room and yell, "I'm under it!"

If you meet big stars—say Leo DiCaprio—give him a Dodger hat and tell him to go away.

And if George Steinbrenner shows up, throw yourself on the floor and say, "George, what happened?"

I know you're gonna do great for the Dodgers. If you don't always have winning seasons, don't worry—you can always go back to your old job tying up boats in Capri.

Your pal,

"Mr. Baseball"

Snoop Dogg
Long Beach, California

Dear Snoop,

We've never met, so I thought I would drop you a line. Why? Because I respect your talent. Your music is from a different generation than mine, but you're still a legend and a big hit with the kids these days. As for the gangster rap, I'm all for it as long as you don't hurt my family.

That said, why "Snoop Dogg"? I don't know whether to throw you a bone or ask you to roll over. When I come to your show, don't ask me to stand on a chair and yell, "Here, Snoop, here Snoop!" With my luck, you'll come over and lift your leg—and that's trouble.

Love ya, you crazy rapper,

RICKLES'
LETTERS
69

Kobe Bryant
Staples Center, Los Angeles

Dear Kobe,

I'm a fan.

That said, stop dribbling around the living room, put down the basketball, and listen to me:

1. Give Jerry Buss a call once in a while—he needs some attention and is exhausted from driving the Brinks truck to your house every morning.
2. Tell Phil Jackson if he wants to relax, forget Zen meditation for a minute, go to Bulgaria, and find an eight-foot center.
3. What's with you guys and all the tattoos? Enough already—you look like a bunch of freeway maps.

RICKLES'
LETTERS
71

4. If you have an extra $45 million, Shaq needs a partner for the sardine-packing plant he's building in Bergen, Norway.

Anyway, that's it, Kobe. Meanwhile, I'm patiently waiting for my $14 million floor seats next to Nicholson—or did you forget?

Sincerely,

DON
RICKLES
72

DON
RICKLES

LOS ANGELES, CALIFORNIA

Michael Bloomberg
Mayor of the City of New York
City Hall, New York, New York

Dear Mayor Bloomberg,

You're doing a damn fine job running the city of New
York. Why? Nobody dresses like you. Just one problem—the
slacks are a little too high in the crotch.

When you stand on the steps of Gracie Mansion, the
crowd chants "Bloomberg! Bloomberg! Bloomberg!" A
couple of dummies yell out, "Koch! Koch! Koch!" but what
do they know?

Okay, I think I've blown enough smoke up the old
chimney, now let's get down to business. The traffic is a
real problem. Have you ever tried to catch a cab during rush
hour? The only way is to throw your kid's carriage in front

of one of 'em. As for the taxi driver, I don't mind if he's wearing a turban, but does he have to sit there with a snake and a basket? Then there's the problem of conversation. As you know, I speak English—I tell him, "Waldorf-Astoria," and he says, "Okay, boss, we go to Chinatown."

Of course, there's always the pleasure of a stroll in Central Park, but that brings up another problem. Yesterday, I went for a walk just as two pigeons circled above me and answered the call of duty—one on each shoulder. Suddenly, at age eighty-two, I looked like a five-star general.

Finally, I invited my cousin Sylvia for a buggy ride through the park, which I thought would be memorable. It was, but only because every time the driver cracked his whip, he smacked Sylvia in the face.

Now they're dating.

Before closing, Mayor, I have to say just a couple words about the restaurants, especially the delis, where the eight-foot-high pastrami sandwiches keep the paramedics busy. Then there's the Italian joints where the waiter serves the spaghetti—half on your plate, half on your pants—followed by the salami, the veal, the parmesan, the bread, the olive oil, the eggplant, the cannolis . . . and what happens after that? The same three paramedics from the deli show up. Finally, there's the French restaurants, but the prices are

ridiculous and that's just for the gravy and a napkin. So forget about it.

For my part, Mayor, I'm going to the hot dog stand in front of the Waldorf Towers.

Yours for a better city,

Don Rickles

P.S.—Not to upset you, Mayor, but I noticed a small leak in the Holland Tunnel, and you might want to check it out. I was driving through and I noticed Ernest Borgnine standing by the crack, yelling, "Everybody put on your life jackets and head for New Jersey!"

Howard Stern
Sirius Satellite Radio
New York, New York

Dear Howard,

I'm sorry, but I can't listen to you anymore. I'm still
a fan, it's just that my Aunt Hilda thinks the Sirius radio
network is connected with Syria and she doesn't want to
hear anything bad about Israel.

So whenever I get out of the house, I never miss the
chance to catch your show. I'm happy to see that your
style and honesty still capture the minds of the young and
institutionalized.

Now, about your head of hair. Howard, I hear that
underneath it all you're a handsome man. Now with a better
nose job, you'll be a real winner.

As to this $20 billion a year you're making, I hear you

bought a house in the Hamptons for $19 billion . . . and that's without a wing for your oh-my-God-look-what-he's-doing-to-her-now movie theater. By the way, I still have nightmares about that one you showed me where your pal Charlie bangs a deer.

Take care, Howard, and continued success with your shortwave radio show.

Your friend and
occasional listener,

DON
RICKLES
78

From the desk of Don Rickles

Dear Jesus,

I'm impressed. For a guy who began as a neighborhood rabbi to start a whole new religion? Wow—now that's an accomplishment. Except, thanks to you, every spring I have to dress up my grandkids so their Gentile friends can hit them with pink-and-blue Easter eggs. The parents sit on the lawn and think it's a million laughs.

Well, Jesus, I hear those church bells ringing. Time for you to get back to work.

Sincerely,

Santa Claus
The North Pole

Dear Santa Claus,

I haven't had a chance to drive up to the North Pole yet, but I have been working some of the Eskimo casinos nearby, so I just might drop in someday soon.

How's your reindeer—Donner and Blitzen and the other cockamamie names that they have? Are you getting 'em ready for Christmas Eve? This time, don't load the sled so heavy or you'll give those reindeer hernias.

Meanwhile, when you don't show up at my house, I've got to face my grandkids and tell 'em, "Don't worry—on Hanukkah I'll double the toys."

Well, keep in touch, Santa. If you run out of winter

underwear—the kind with the fly in front—give me a call. My cousin Saul can get 'em for you wholesale. In the meantime, kiss my jingle bells.

Ho-ho-ho,

Don Rickles

Julius Caesar
The Forum
Rome, Italy

Dear Jules,

I didn't know you personally, but I had an uncle from
back in those days who was in the toga business and told me
all about you.

He said you liked your togas tight around the ass with
just a little give in the stomach. Even without the rope, he
said the fit drove the girls crazy.

You should know that you were his favorite customer,
Julie. That's why it broke his heart when you took your
business to Brooks Brothers after they opened a shop in
downtown Rome. Uncle Max went broke—how could you
do that to the struggling little guy?

Even after that, Max loved you. Still, it always bothered

him that you took a hundred of your best oarsmen and had 'em row your barge around the Bay of Naples, yelling "Row! Row! Row!" just so you could pop his wife's best friend's kid sister, Lilly.

Those must have been the days, Jules. Too bad I missed 'em. By the time I got to Rome with my wife, Barbara, and Aunt Rifka, all that was left of you was a discount shoe store across from the Trevi Fountain. Still, they were doing brisk business with your original style of open-toe sandals. I guess that when in Rome, it's still "Hail Caesar, the shoe salesman."

Yours truly,

Al Donte

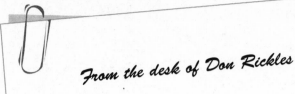

My dear Moses,

Could I use you today! There's a number of talented magicians out there, but no real miracle workers. Your Red Sea trick is first-class and the burning bush bit is a showstopper.

I know a true professional like yourself never tells his secrets, but how in God's name do you do it? Freeing the Jews from Egypt without buses, cars, or bikes—that took some planning. And when you came down the mountain with the Tylenol tablets just in time to stop everyone from dressing up like rhinos and squirrels and building the world's first Jew zoo? Even I gotta thank you for that one.

Anyway, I gotta go. I know you're busy planning an appearance at the synagogue in New Rochelle, but

 *From the desk of Don Rickles*

think about this: With me as your promoter, we'd make more noise than The Beatles.

Just look what you did for Charlton Heston.

Your future business partner,

DON
RICKLES
86

God

Heaven

Dear God,

I love you and I respect you so I'm not about to get cute with the wisecracks. Besides, at eighty-two that could be shaky.

Look what you've done for me: a beautiful wife, children, grandchildren, and loving friends. The sense of humor you've given me has taken me a long way. Who would have thought there was money in telling a guy in a Vegas audience, "Take off your hat, it's not a Jewish holiday."

RICKLES'
LETTERS
87

Thinking along those lines, is there any chance of getting me better seats for the High Holidays?

Either way, I'll be there.

Love,

Arnold Palmer
Latrobe, Pennsylvania

Dear Arnie,

I haven't heard from you since we were together at an awards dinner in Vegas. That was the night I said you had a face like a 9-iron. I can't remember if you laughed. If not, I got over it.

But who am I to put you down, Arnie? You've got Arnie's Army. Those guys are nuts. They collect the towels you use to wipe your practice balls.

You're a legend, Arnie, but retirement was smart. Your tee shot became a dribbler. Now I see pictures of you sitting on your tractor in a godforsaken field in the middle of

RICKLES'
LETTERS
89

Pennsylvania. Get a farm, Arnie, learn to work the tractor and open a little smoked salmon stand on the highway. With your luck, it'll be a big hit.

Yours truly,

Tiger Woods
Windermere, Florida

Dear Tiger,

Great name. Had it been Pussycat, you might have wound up an attendant at a cat and dog hospital.

No one has branded himself better than you. You're a spokesperson for watches, cars, shoes, tennis courts, golf courses, islands . . . next you'll be selling land on Indian casino reservations.

By the way, I played a little golf in my time. I remember the day I found myself at the club, teamed up with Evel Knievel. Our opponents were Milton Berle and Ray Bolger. My tee shot was magnificent. My second shot was great. But my third shot had me living up to my nickname: "Out-

of-Bounds Rickles." Evel and I ended up playing the parts of Lewis and Clark, hunting the woods in search of my ball.

Good thing Evel was betting against me.

You don't have that problem, Tiger. You're to golf what Sophie Tucker was to singing.

You both have the same swing.

Your fan,

DON
RICKLES
92

DON
RICKLES
LOS ANGELES, CALIFORNIA

"Dear Abby" Newspaper Column
U.S.A.

Dear Abby,

Give it a rest. I really don't need your advice. My family
and I are in good shape. But that doesn't stop me from
reading your column.

For instance, I loved the story about the guy who walked
around with his zipper down. I agreed with you when you
told him, "If it makes you comfortable, fine, but close it up
on holidays."

I also loved the advice you gave the lady who fell in love
with the captain of the Staten Island Ferry: "Stop talking to
him in Norwegian; he used to be the leading tango dancer in
Buenos Aires."

But my favorite piece of advice was what you told the

RICKLES'
LETTERS
93

eighty-five-year-old bachelor: "Eat as much as you want—
and more. I saw the cardiogram. You got about a month."

Best,

Brett Favre
Gulfport, Mississippi

Dear Brett,

I'm a football fan. I loved Bobby Layne, I loved Johnny U, I loved Broadway Joe.

But none of those guys knew how to catch a catfish.

Still, I'm sure you're going to be the toast of the town, Brett. Breakfast at Tiffany's, lunch at the Astor, and if you ever have any trouble getting dinner reservations at the Latin Quarter, feel free to call me.

If it all doesn't work out in New York, take your pads, your helmet, your wife, and your private jet, and fly back to

RICKLES'
LETTERS
95

Mississippi to what you do best: blowing up footballs without a pump.

Your fan,

David Beckham
Beverly Hills, California

Dear David,

Sorry, but I just don't understand your game. I know it's the most popular sport in the world, but what's the big deal about guys running around some oversized lawn in their underwear?

Every time I see you and your Spice Girl wife strolling around Beverly Hills, you're yelling, "Goooooooooooooooooooooooooooooooal!!!"

Get off it! You're not the only star in town.

I actually went to a soccer match and enjoyed it. Watching two guys leap high in the air, bumping heads, and falling unconscious deserves a standing ovation. The point system was equally exciting—to sit there for twenty

hours just to see a 0-0 score was a thrill. And when the fans, looking for even more excitement, started rioting, that was the best part of the day.

I'll be back, only this time I'm bringing my pit bull.

Heads up,

DON
RICKLES

President Jimmy Carter
Plains, Georgia

Dear President Carter,

Enough with the peanuts.

Enough with polishing up your Nobel Prize.

Enough with ending world poverty.

Forget your hammer and nails and Habitat House and read my book.

You could use a good laugh, especially since there's no chance you'll be reelected.

Stay where you are in Plains, Georgia, because, believe me, you'd never be comfortable in a condo in Miami Beach.

Yours truly,

Letters to People Who Are Important but Don't Want to Know Me

DON
RICKLES
LOS ANGELES, CALIFORNIA

Oprah Winfrey
The Oprah Winfrey Show
Harpo Productions, Chicago, Illinois

Dear Oprah,

There's a rumor going around that you're going to buy the United States. I have a big favor to ask: Could my wife and I be in on it?

Anyway, we're big fans. We watch you every afternoon. Well, not every afternoon, but a lot. Okay, maybe once a month. Actually, she watches and I nod and agree.

Whatever the case, we're always amazed at your great kindness to give every audience member who comes to the show either a car or a ship. Some people even get a guest house with a lawn and trees.

Anyway, I've been meaning to drop you a line for a while

RICKLES'
LETTERS
103

now, just to say congratulations. You're powerful, you're rich, and you've got a big, generous heart. Not to mention the house in Santa Barbara that's worth more than Canada.

Oprah, dear—you take care. I wish you nothing but continued success. And if by some miracle I pass in your thoughts, a Maserati in blue would be a wonderful surprise.

Your biggest fan,

Don Rickles

Dr. Phil McGraw
Beverly Hills, California

Dear Dr. Phil,

Watched the show the other day, and boy was I impressed. For a simple guy (and I mean that with all due respect), you sure know everything about everything.

I love the part where you take some poor dazed guy staring off into space and tell him you can make him normal. That's your genius, Doc, 'cause you and I both know he's never gonna get better.

How do you find all these sick people?

Do you ever go home at night, lie on the couch, and say, "What's wrong with *me*? Can I really be perfect?"

Sincerely,

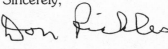

RICKLES'
LETTERS
105

DON
RICKLES
LOS ANGELES, CALIFORNIA

Donald Trump
Chairman and CEO
The Trump Organization
Top of the Trump Tower

Dear Donald,

If I hear your name one more time, I'm going to run Regis into traffic.

But in all sincerity, we go way back. From my early days performing for you and all the Trump relatives in both Long Island and Florida, I think of you as family. I know that you've been busy, but you'll be glad to know that I'm still breathing.

But let's talk business. I'm all for you turning the Statue of Liberty into lofts for the Wall Street kids. Same goes for Grand Central Station. While you're at it, I think your idea

RICKLES'
LETTERS
107

to turn the Amazon rain forest into a theme park is a dandy. If my vote counts, I say you call it Trumpland.

Why not, Don? The world is your oyster. You're a master of marketing. It's almost scary how you put your face on everything you own. Why, last time I played Mar-a-Lago, I couldn't help but notice the Trump face everywhere I looked. There you were, smiling at me from the logo on the stage floor during my performance. After the show, I asked for a bottle of water at the bar and who was staring at me from the label? You, Donald. And at the end of the night I pulled back the shower curtain, and there you were in the tub with two toy ducks and your new wife.

Best,

The Other Don

Dear Madonna,

Congratulations—you're world-renowned.
And why?
Is it the singing? Ehh, not bad . . .
Is it the dancing? . . . So-so, but I don't think so.
So what is it about you that gets everyone?
It's gotta be your hot Kabbalahs.

My best,

Don Rickles

RICKLES'
LETTERS
109

Don King
Las Vegas, Nevada

Dear Don,

Just a note to let you know I spoke to the United Barbers Alliance: Two barbers recently had fatal heart attacks trying to chop down your forest. But keep smiling, Don. You got a great dentist.

Yours for good grooming,

Don Rickles

Rupert Murdoch
News Corp.
New York, New York

Dear Rupert,

Other people in Beverly Hills get the *New York Times* delivered daily. I get the *New York Post*. Why? Because I like your paper, especially Page Six. It tells me everything about everything, and I wind up knowing nothing, like how Lindsay Lohan is giving up sex for driving lessons.

As a loyal *Post* reader, I have just one little gripe: Can you dump the sex and run more stories about jai alai in Miami?

Best,

RICKLES'
LETTERS
113

Fidel Castro
Havana, Cuba

Dear Fidel,

I hear you're retiring to start a rumba band. If you
need a good bongo player, call my cousin Lupe. He's got a
bicycle shop outside downtown Havana, and when it comes
to the bongos, he's the man. If you can't get him, get John
Stamos, a great drummer. I'm sure he'll go for the airfare to
Cuba.

Tell me the truth: You're not really going to let your
brother run the country, are you? Does he know you keep
all the ammo at your house?

I'm not going to take up any more of your time because
I know you've got to take a nap. But be smart, Fidel. Don't

RICKLES'
LETTERS
115

let your brother give you any sleeping pills unless he takes them first.

Kiss my Ambien,

Don Rickles

DON
RICKLES
LOS ANGELES, CALIFORNIA

Mayor Antonio Villaraigosa
City Hall, Los Angeles

Dear Mayor Villaraigosa,

Our city is in trouble, and I've got some advice.

Give the Koreans crash helmets or signs for their cars that read, GET OUT OF THE WAY, I'M COMING!

Now that you're mayor, give the Latinos what they deserve: plenty of rest and Dodgers season tickets.

There's no question you've helped the city. You're doing great things. But I got a little suspicious when I learned that you went down to the border and signaled from the fence with your flashlight: one blink for a maid, two blinks for a bellhop, and three blinks for a cook and a busboy. I hope you have a sense of humor, Mayor, otherwise I'll have to hide out in Britney Spears's laundry.

RICKLES'
LETTERS
117

As for the rest of the city, all of Hollywood is at your call, Mayor: booze, broads, parties, porno movies. It's the perfect training ground to prepare you for a run for President of the United States.

Your possible voter,

Don Rickles

Letters to My Friends in Heaven

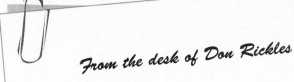

From the desk of Don Rickles

Dear Charlton Heston,

I miss you, Mister Heston.

Just a quick update from down here: They're talking about giving you your own holiday. Once a year, on your birthday, everyone in America would get a rifle and start the hunt.

I hope everything's A-OK up in your big chariot in the sky. Maybe now God can get you and the real Moses together, and the two of you can work up a couple of new miracles . . . like getting me some more concert dates down here.

Whatever you do, try to keep it down in heaven. Riding around in a chariot through some of those quiet neighborhoods and yelling, "See my movies!" isn't something Chuck Heston should do.

Sincerely,

RICKLES'
LETTERS
121

From the desk of Don Rickles

Dear Elvis,

You are gone, but still the king, and the whole world knows it.

Last time I was in Memphis, I had the pleasure of visiting Graceland. Now Elvis, I gotta be honest: you might have been the greatest rock and roller, but when it came to interior decoration you had guitar damage. Your living room is done up in dead tiger, your kitchen is early–Holiday Inn, and they wouldn't let us upstairs to see the master bedroom because there were a couple of girls still waiting for you.

Then I went across the street to the souvenir shop. The Elvis ashtrays were nice, the salt-and-pepper shakers were classy, but the miniature toilets were too much.

Fortunately, you passed away before your hips gave out.

Your forever fan,

RICKLES'
LETTERS
123

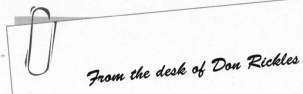

From the desk of Don Rickles

Dear Marilyn Monroe,

God bless you, sweetheart. I know you had a hard time down here, and I hope things are easier for you now. Even though you're out of your body, I still get excited when I think about you. I know that because my leg goes up.

Marilyn, your voice was always a knockout, and I miss it. I try to duplicate it by sitting in the closet and talking low into a coffee cup, but unfortunately it still doesn't do anything for my leg.

Yours truly,

Don Rickles

P.S.—Do they have subway grates in heaven, or do the guys just put mirrors on their shoes?

From the desk of Don Rickles

Dear Lucy,

A lot of female comics have come and gone, but there will never be another Lucille Ball. I'll never forget the time I did your television show: I knew you were going to be tough on me right from the start.

How?

You came to greet me wearing leather boots and carrying a whip.

Then there was your wonderful five-word directing technique, ringing out from the back of the soundstage:

"You are wrong, Mister Rickles!"

But that's okay, Lucy. You earned the right to be the boss . . . . especially with the help of the musically-inclined Cuban fellow. But let's be honest: His bongo playing was great, but how many babaloos can a guy take? Why didn't you just turn him over to immigration?

As ever,

From the desk of Don Rickles

Dear Howard Cosell,

Monday nights are not the same without you. Every time I turned on the game, I always learned a lot about you—too bad you never had any interest in talking about the two teams playing.

Who could forget all those wonderful times Muhammad Ali tried to pull off your toupee on national TV. What were you hiding under there? His draft card? Howard, honestly, your toupee looked like a dead beaver rejected by Larry, Moe, and Curly.

Remember all our great times at the Friars Club? Your introductions were so terrific you set my career back ten years. But I'm not angry. I'm not bitter. I love you Howard, but when you went to heaven, I had to agree with your agent's remark: "Not everyone's gonna miss him."

Your friend,

Don Rickles

RICKLES'
LETTERS
129

From the desk of Don Rickles

Dear Frank,

Boy, do I miss you. All my Sinatra memories are really swinging around in my head today. I'm holding a ticket from the Crystal Room at the Desert Inn, December, 1992. Written on it:

THE VOICE AND THE MOUTH . . .
TOGETHER ON STAGE

The two of us, Frank, performing together. "What an honor," I told the crowd that night, "to be opening for the greatest singer of all time." Of course, one of your boys had a gun on me from the wings, but I would have said it regardless.

After the show, we went to dinner, just you, me, and Jilly. When the waiter leaned over too far with the bread, you shoved him halfway across the room and the whole joint started laughing . . . it was safer that way.

Then there was the night in Cannes when you were good enough to invite me to dinner.

RICKLES'
LETTERS
131

From the desk of Don Rickles

"Order the escargot du chevalier," you told me.

"I don't like escargot," I told you.

"Trust me, Don. The escargot here are out of this world."

When the escargot arrived, they looked like the chef had sat on them.

I took a bite. My stomach left town.

"How about you, Frank?" I asked. "You haven't touched your escargot."

"I'm not eating that crap." Frank laughed as he pushed his plate away.

Jilly laughed even louder.

Speaking of Jilly, is he still chasing after you in heaven, or does he have an after-life of his own? I'm kidding. I loved Jilly almost as much as I loved you, Frank, in spite of his threatening to tell you that Dean Martin is fed up with your tomato sauce.

And Frank, the whole mob thing was blown way out of proportion. Just because you know where Jimmy Hoffa is buried doesn't make you a bad guy.

From the desk of Don Rickles

So put your dreams away for another day. There'll never be another you. But now that you're gone, I have no problem telling you that Dick Haymes always had the better voice. (He wished.)

Love,

Don

From the desk of Don Rickles

Dear President Reagan,

I write this with a sentimental heart. To have performed at your inauguration is something I will never forget.

I did have some problems with the Secret Service, though. They wanted to know if my Uncle Jack ran around Jones Beach screaming, "I'm a clam! Open me!" I also couldn't explain why my cousin Emma rode down Flatbush Avenue yelling, "Liberace was my lover!"

Ronnie, you were great on *General Electric Theater*. But it was a shame when they replaced you with a light bulb.

With great respect,
Mister President,

RICKLES'
LETTERS
135

From the desk of Don Rickles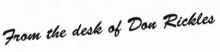

Dear John Wayne,

They don't make 'em like you anymore: slow walking and slower talking. I still love all your movies, especially the ones where you climb all over Maureen O'Hara.

Things aren't the same without you, Duke. Back in your day, you really knew how to ride a horse. Today's kids have a problem getting on a bike.

I guess it's time for you to ride into the sunset. I'll wait down here. If a cattle drive comes through, Duke, how do I reach you?

Sincerely,

From the desk of Don Rickles

Dear Julia Child,

I had to write you when I learned that you were a spy for our side in the Office of Strategic Services during World War II.

I know you did a great job poisoning our enemies with your boiled beef stew. And your salted sausages made the Germans go blind.

You were the cook of cooks. Only you could stuff a dead chicken: You could stick your right thumb in, shove it all the way up to the mouth, and still make the bird smile. You were the height of style and grace, even if your voice could have closed the Metropolitan Opera and your posture would have gotten you kicked out of West Point.

Bon appetit,

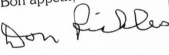

RICKLES'
LETTERS
139

From the desk of Don Rickles

Dear Babe,

Everybody claims they were at the ballpark the day you hit your sixtieth home run, but I actually *was* there. My uncle Saul told me we had great seats, but we were so high up in the bleachers, pilots waved at us.

Didn't matter. It was still a thrill. As the game went on, over the loudspeaker came the words, "NUMBER THREE . . . BABE RUTH!" I got so excited that my pants dropped off and fell three rows past the guy hawking cotton candy.

Suddenly a tremendous crack of the bat. Then a screeching sound. As I saw the ball zooming right at me, I knew this could be the souvenir of a lifetime. Unfortunately, I forgot my glove, so I hid under Uncle Saul. But he ducked, and the next thing I knew I was at Presbyterian Hospital mumbling, "Where's the Babe?"

From the desk of Don Rickles

Hope this true story amuses you as you lounge on a fluffy cloud, eating a Baby Ruth.

Your biggest fan,

Don Rickles

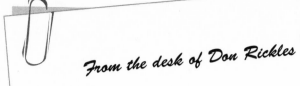 *From the desk of Don Rickles*

Dear Milton,

As a teenager, you were my idol. Your wit, your timing—Milton Berle had it all.

As the years passed, I was lucky enough to become your friend. That's when I saw it was time to look for another idol.

I remember those days in New York when you held court at Lindy's. If anyone interrupted you, you'd force him to sit at Henny Youngman's table.

My mother adored you, and of course you adored her chopped liver, even though it gave you heartburn.

You always gave me advice, Milton, and when I took it, you said it was wrong.

Whenever we went out for lunch, you were the star. My job was to hand you the silverware.

Your fellow trooper,

RICKLES'
LETTERS
143

From the desk of Don Rickles

Dear Joe Louis,

You were my first boxing hero. You made Americans proud. You were Detroit's Brown Bomber. You never flew a mission over Germany, but you dropped the bomb on Max Schmeling.

A lifetime later, I got to know you when we both worked Vegas. Every time I'd go up to you, I'd say, "Better watch it, Champ, I'm gonna drop you." And you always said, "Don, how's your mother?"

There have been other champs. Mike Tyson was great until he mistook Holyfield's ear for a hot dog. Then there was Marvin Hagler, Tommy Hearns, and Sugar Ray Leonard. Now they're all retired—Marvin moved to France, where he became curator at a museum of medieval religious art. Hitman Hearns became an advisor to the atomic energy program. And Sugar Ray retired to play the tuba for an oom-pa-pa band in a subway station in Warsaw, Poland.

 *From the desk of Don Rickles*

They were all great champs. But the man who won the hearts of the American people was you, Joe. You'll never be knocked out.

Your fan,

Don

Letters from My Travels Around the World

DON
RICKLES
LOS ANGELES, CALIFORNIA

Minister of Chinese Tourism
Beijing, China

Dear Minister,

I just got back from visiting your country and I thought you might like to know my thoughts:

First, there's too many people on the streets. They're on bicycles, motorcycles, buses, and trains; they're coming out of the manholes—they're everywhere! There's so many people, the cops have to stand on boxes to direct traffic—either improve the stoplights or get taller cops.

Here's my point: that one-kid-per-family rule isn't working. Maybe half-a-kid-per-family, Mr. Minister . . . think about it.

Second, why'd you have to make the Great Wall so damn long? Climbing it was a real kick, but there should be

RICKLES'
LETTERS
149

a doctor's office halfway up offering free mouth-to-mouth. I was lucky to be traveling with my friend Leonard Steinman, head of cardiology at a small hospital in Encino. Otherwise I'd still be up there.

The countryside is beautiful, dotted with straw hats. Most of the farmers are bent over, planting rice. (On a side note, a chiropractor could make a killing in China.) But why are some people still walking around in their pajamas? For all the clothes you guys make these days, can't you see to it that a couple pairs of pants fall off every cargo boat?

As I write to you, I'm in Shanghai. It's a lovely city and a lot like New York—especially the air pollution—except I can't get a decent plate of chow mein anywhere. You should send for a few New York Chinatown cooks with a couple of pots and a rice strainer.

Yours truly,

Don Rickles

DON
RICKLES

LOS ANGELES, CALIFORNIA

Queen Elizabeth II
Buckingham Palace
London, England

Your Majesty,

Thank you for inviting me and the missus to the palace this past Saturday for a lovely evening dinner banquet—what an honor. Okay, so the booze was a bit weak and the hors d'oeuvres were nothing to talk about, but the main course of boar's head cooked in Manischewitz wine was quite interesting.

As for the festivities: no offense, but I probably would have done it different. At dancing time, every number was a waltz and the old men were so bent-over they were smelling their shoes.

But don't think that we aren't grateful. Next time you're

in Los Angeles, look us up—we'd love to take you to a jewelry show so you can get something nice.

Respectfully,

DON
RICKLES
LOS ANGELES, CALIFORNIA

His Holiness Pope Benedict XVI
Vatican City
Rome, Italy

Your Holiness,

Thanks for the audience. Met the last pope: you know, the Polish gentleman. Very friendly, even if his kitchen floor was done in bad linoleum. Too bad he didn't have time to go grab a bite to eat, but The Boss called and he had to take it. Before we parted company, I noticed he accidentally left the price tag on his signet ring. It was a little embarrassing, especially when I noticed it had been marked down 50 percent.

Anyhow, I hope you don't make the same mistake. By the way, I had a problem last time I was here. Even though I'm Jewish, I still wanted to go to the Sistine Chapel and say

a prayer. But when I went to light a candle, paint started dripping on my head. So I asked the monsignor: Could this mean trouble for me?

Finally, I have a favor to ask, Holy Father: I don't mean to be pushy, but is there any chance I could work the cardinals' dinner next Easter? I assure you, I work clean. You won't hear a negative word about your faith—I can't chance a massive stroke at my age.

In the meantime, keep me in your prayers and throw in an extra blessing for the Lakers.

Sincerely,

Don Rickles

DON
RICKLES
154

DON
RICKLES
LOS ANGELES, CALIFORNIA

Italian Tourism Minister
Venice, Italy

Dear Mister Minister,

Let me start by saying that Venice is my kind of town. The missus and I just got back from a wonderful vacation.

We had a romantic candlelight dinner in a restaurant along the canal. We spent the whole evening asking the waiter, "Where's that smell coming from?"

Still, the food was unbelievable: The pasta, the bread, the oil, the garlic, the veal, more veal, veal picata, veal parmesan, veal-that, veal-this, veal-on-the-wall, veal-in-the-bathroom, veal everywhere—pick up the tempo and I think we have a hit.

Grazie,

Don

D O N
R I C K L E S
LOS ANGELES, CALIFORNIA

Ambassador to Spain
Madrid, Spain

Dear Mr. Ambassador,

Thank you for inviting Barbara and me to celebrate our wedding anniversary in Madrid. It was also great that you invited the Israeli ambassador. Replacing the paella with whitefish on a cracker was a nice gesture. I also enjoyed the flamenco dancing you provided as entertainment, even though we had to throw cold water on the guy and gal to separate them.

The next day, you treated us to ringside seats at the bullfight. We were so close to the action the matador handed me his cape and hat. But then the bull charged and the matador leaped over the barrier and said, "I'll stay with the wife. You fight the bull."

Ole!

RICKLES'
LETTERS
157

DON
RICKLES

Minister of Russian Tourism
The Kremlin
Moscow, Russia

Dear Boris,

    I know everything has changed since the missus and
I visited your country over twenty years ago. And I do
appreciate your invitation to make me grand marshal of the
caviar-throwing tournament. But I must decline because my
cousin's sister's aunt's niece got the measles.

    Only last week, my wife and I went down Memory Lane
and recalled our wonderful vacation to the former USSR.
The brochure said five-star all the way, but when they gave
us a room with an army cot and a toilet with no chain we
weren't exactly thrilled.

    Before that, when I got off the elevator, I found myself

face-to-face with a female security guard who looked like she had run into a wall. She had a chain of keys dangling from her neck to the floor, which might have had something to do with her hump. I didn't know why she was there until she said, "Turn over all your belongings."

The next evening, my wife and I went to the ballet. As we sat in our box seats, I said, "Do you get the feeling this place smells from herring?" During the opening pirouette, two of the ballerinas screwed themselves into the ground.

As we were leaving the theater, a guard came over and whispered to me, "I have a dead uncle in Detroit. Could you go out to his grave and leave him some flowers?"

"Sure thing," I said.

As I walked away, he said, "Wait! You don't know the address!"

I kept walking.

A couple of days later, we flew to the magnificent city of St. Petersburg. It was an interesting flight. Every five minutes the cockpit door flew open and the pilot yelled, "We're gonna try to land!"

When we finally *did* land, we made our way to the Hermitage. The paintings of the exotic birds were so realistic that they flew off the canvas and swooped down over us. We hit the floor, thinking it was a bombing raid.

After the all-clear signal, one of the curators promised
to mail us a one-of-a-kind portrait of Stalin after a shower
with his bathrobe open.

Then it was off to dinner. Buckets of caviar, sardines
with their eyes open, and special vodka imported from
Hong Kong. After the meal, I felt a little queasy. Barbara
called for the hotel doctor, but when two nurses carrying
a straightjacket broke down the door, I suddenly felt much
better and asked them to leave.

Looking forward to
my next visit (but don't wait
for me at the airport),

Letters About Things I Need to Get Off My Chest

DON
RICKLES
LOS ANGELES, CALIFORNIA

American Academy of Dramatic Arts
120 Madison Ave.
New York, NY 10016

Dear American Academy of Dramatic Arts,

Hi, it's Don Rickles—class of 1950—the greatest student you guys ever turned out.

Forget Grace Kelly, Don Murray, Tom Poston, Jason Robards, and Anne Bancroft—let's get down to the nitty-gritty.

I'm the guy who played Mr. Potato Head.

Now that's talent!

So I hope you honor my request to build a small statue of me. Nothing gigantic, but I would like it to be life-size. If it's not asking too much, it should also be placed in the main hall, arms outstretched, inviting in more eager young minds.

RICKLES'
LETTERS
165

Recently a young artist asked me for a recommendation to the Academy. I said, "Kid, acting is a tough career. Look what happened to me."

Yours theatrically,

Don Rickles

DON
RICKLES

LOS ANGELES, CALIFORNIA

National Hockey League Commissioner
Hockeyville, Canada

Dear NHL Commissioner,

Just a note to let you know: I'm not upset, but I'm starting to lose my mind. I've got a garage full of hockey pucks and it's gotten so far out of control that my housekeeper has flooded the basement and made a rink.

I never played hockey as a kid and the only time I watch it on TV is when I can't fall asleep.

Don't get me wrong: hockey is a great sport if you don't mind winding up with ice burns on your ass. You never hear, "Now starting at goalie for the New York Rangers, Larry Lipshitz!"

So under separate cover I'm sending you two thousand hockey pucks. I'm keeping the one "Boom Boom"

RICKLES'
LETTERS
167

Geoffrion autographed for me one night after I did a show in Montreal, though. It has sentimental value and it works great as a doorstop.

Sincerely,

Don Rickles

Dear Paris,

Don't get nervous—I'm a fan. Why? Because you're beautiful, smart, and you know how to carry a dog.

Most girls your age must really envy you: You're named after the most glamorous city in the world and your grandfather's empire of luxury hotels. Just thank God your name isn't Hoboken Howard Johnson.

Paris, I'm concerned about what kind of guy you're going to end up with. Whoever he is, he's going to have a hard time competing with the dog and the photographers and your visits to the bank vaults.

Good luck, sweetheart, and do your best to stay out of jail. The police are tired of bringing you takeout from Spago.

Best,

Osama bin Laden
Somewhere in the World
Let's take a wild guess—Pakistan

Dear Osama,

You're becoming a real pain in my ass, way up there in the mountains. Just let me find you a nice condo in downtown Tel Aviv already.

Your trustworthy real estate agent,

RICKLES'
LETTERS
171

DON
RICKLES

Chief Administrator
Cedars-Sinai Medical Center
Los Angeles, California

Dear Mr. Administrator,

I know that hospitals are incredibly important and that nothing is perfect, but I gotta say something about my last visit:

Morning.

Five A.M.

I'm in a deep sleep. Let's call it a coma.

In comes the nurse, pulls back the sheet and stares at my magnificent body. All I can do is pray she doesn't touch the basic toys.

Next, sponge bath time. I'm an excitable guy: up and down the arms and across the chest is okay, but when she goes down to the village area, I tend to stiffen up. And

RICKLES'
LETTERS
173

before I've had time to relax, she rolls me over and washes me across the valley of death. It's all well and good, but do the other nurses have to take pictures?

When breakfast arrives, I take one look and say, "Put me on the critical list."

Lunch and dinner could hurt. I ask the nurse to taste it first. When she does and her shoes turn up, I know it's trouble.

So I spend the rest of the day competing in the bedpan roller derby up and down the hall.

My best to the staff. See you next time, hopefully as a visitor.

Sincerely,

Don Rickles

Letters to My Friends Who Talk Too Much

Barbara Walters
The View
ABC-TV
New York, New York

Dear Barbara,

I'm writing to thank you for your friendship. It all began
at Westbury theater, many years ago. So many years, that
the Long Island Railroad wasn't even finished. I was coming
off stage, where I'd just told a woman in the front row,
"Take off the mask—Halloween's over."

I turned around and there you were. I thought I was
looking at Lois Lane.

"No," you told me, "it's Barbara Walters."

"Of course it's you," I said. "These cataracts are driving
me crazy." That's when our friendship began. It didn't
matter that you never put me on any of your TV specials. It

RICKLES'
LETTERS
177

didn't matter that it took forever to have me on that show of yours where the women don't stop talking.

I could never be angry with you, Barbara, because I was one of the guys who used to go to your father's fabulous nightclub, the Latin Quarter.

I went on leave as a young sailor during World War II. One particular night, I was with a couple of young ladies and a buddy. Ted Lewis and his clarinet were on stage. Great show, great booze, great food. I was doing great until the check came. Chest pain circled my heart. But everything turned out okay—one of the girls gave me mouth-to-mouth.

Barbara, getting back to you. I've got to be honest, I don't have a lot to say to you. You have a very attractive wardrobe, but the day you came out wearing the little girl sailor suit wasn't you. If you have a problem with your wardrobe, call my aunt in the Bronx—she's the best seamstress on Jerome Avenue. Just mention me and I'm sure she'll give you a good price.

Love,

Don

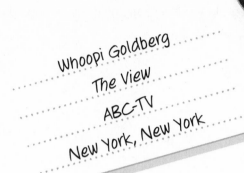

Whoopi Goldberg
The View
ABC-TV
New York, New York

Dear Whoopi,

The first time I heard your name, I thought you were a hockey star. Then I found out you were a brilliant comedian. You won my heart over when you adopted two needy children, Billy Crystal and Robin Williams, whom you groomed into fine young men.

Now that you're on *The View,* I have some advice: Kiss up to Barbara; she's the money. And when you get the raise you so richly deserve, I'm taking you to Diana Lubowitz, one of the finest dressmakers in New York. She'll come up with a fine new *shmata* for you. It'll be a whole new look and with any luck we'll see you in *Vogue.*

By the way, thank you for your kind remarks about me

in my HBO documentary. I hope they do one on you next.
I'd love to return the favor and say nice things about you,
but I just don't have the time.

Love,

Don

Women of The View
WABC-TV
New York, New York

Dear Women of *The View,*

I love the show and watch you guys every day. Why? Because hearing a studio full of women yell and scream is a great way to start a prison break.

Your conversations are attention-grabbing. For example: The one about the cattle industry getting meatloaf shots really got my appetite going. Then there was Tom Cruise's encore of his *Oprah* performance, when he did three cartwheels and a back handspring over a car.

I also enjoyed your interview with George Clooney, especially when all of you started ripping off your clothes and yelling, "Why not me?"

Anyway, keep up the great work. I wish you all

continued success and look forward to seeing you all at the next women's wrestling convention.

Love,

Regis Philbin
New York, New York

Dear Reg,

We go as far back as Noah's Ark.

Who was the one who told you *Password* would fly? *Me!*

Who was the one who said the *Millionaire* show would be a hit? *Me!*

And when Joey Bishop was about to give you a nervous breakdown, who took the gun out of your mouth? *Me!*

Reg, I'm a little concerned. It's time for you to take down the Dean Martin shrine in your living room where you kneel and sing "That's Amore."

By the way, I'm glad you've become such close friends with Donald Trump, especially since he's named you the new night manager at Mar-a-Lago.

RICKLES'
LETTERS
183

That's all, Reg. I've got to go tell David Letterman,
"Enough with the Regis jokes! Promote me for a change!"

Your pal,

Mr. David Letterman
The Late Show
New York, New York

Dear Dave,

How's my guy? You're Mr. Social. You're Charlie Cocktail Party. You run around town from one big-shot dinner to another.

The truth is that you never go out.

Do you have some sort of secret hideaway? I've known you for twenty-five years. You're always cordial, you're always friendly. At times you're even funny.

But who are you, Dave? How are you? Why are you?

I have no idea. No one knows. You get to the show five minutes before it starts and you're outta there five minutes after it's over.

What are you, Batman? Some say you live in a

treehouse on Staten Island. Others say you have a small room in the back of a grocery store in Brooklyn, where your food is delivered in sealed containers and tested beforehand by Paul Shaffer.

I understand privacy, Dave, but don't you think you're pushing it a little?

The reason I'm writing you is simple: Invite me to your home, if there is one. Let's let the world know you're normal. By the way, I'll bring a brisket.

Your friend,

Don

Jimmy Kimmel
Jimmy Kimmel Live!
Hollywood, California

Dear Jimmy,

You're the only Italian kid I know who's got a shot at being a scoutmaster at forty. Jimmy, you're the late-night host's answer to apple pie.

When I first heard of you—how can I put it, Jimmy?—you were a Mickey Mouse sportscaster. Then—boom!—from left field, you were host of a major network show.

Somebody in your family with a lotta juice must have made a phone call.

All in all, I gotta admit that the kid from Vegas did pretty

good. If your ratings take a dip, you can always become a lifeguard at one of Steve Wynn's pools.

Love ya,

Dear Jay,

I'm angry at you.

Last week, there I was driving down Pacific Coast Highway and enjoying the ocean view when suddenly my prized 1969 Corvair blew up on me. Steam was coming out of the engine. Firemen arrived screaming. Cops arrived yelling. Then the Automobile Club arrived with a team of mechanics. For some reason, they were dressed in suits and ties. Someone must have told them there was a wedding. But no one knew what a Corvair was.

"I have a friend," I said. "His hobby is smelling brake fluid. He can fix any car."

"Who is he?" they asked me.

"Jay Leno."

"Jay Leno isn't about to come out and help you."

"Jay's my friend," I said. "Jay will do anything for a friend."

But when I called your office, Jay, they said you were out in the Valley buying up banks. You were too busy figuring out how to get another network to buy you Southern France.

So my Corvair is still sitting there by the side of the road.

When I was waiting for the Number Four bus back to LA, you passed me by on one of your Harley-Davidsons. You tried to wave, but hundred-dollar bills kept flying out of your saddlebags.

Love ya,

Don

Craig Ferguson
The Late Late Show
Hollywood, California

Dear Craig,

I'm writing to give you an alert: Work on your accent. I know you became a U.S. citizen, but after watching many of your shows, immigration is taking another long hard look at your credentials. They're seriously considering pressing charges and sending you back to your native Scotland, where you'll be more comfortable doing your former job herding sheep.

It's amazing how a guy in a kilt got to be a big star. It's kinda odd, though, that the whole audience lays on the floor looking up. From what I've heard, there's not much to see.

Yours truly,

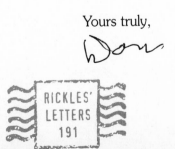

RICKLES'
LETTERS
191

Jon Stewart
The Daily Show
New York, New York

Dear Jon,

I'm writing you because I'm puzzled.

Are you a comic pretending to be a newsman or a newsman pretending to be a comic? Either way, you're in trouble.

One night you're interviewing the head cabana boy at the Jamaica Hilton and the next night you're shooting the breeze with the son-in-law of the president of France's brother.

I gotta level with you, Jon. Your network has thought

of replacing you, but Dick Cavett is busy interviewing the president of France's sister.

Your friend,

Conan O'Brien
Late Night
New York, New York

Dear Conan,

You mesmerize me when you come out for your monologue and start jumping up and down like something just ran up your underwear.

At 7'9", you're an imposing guy, so much so that the audience doesn't know whether to applaud or throw ropes around you.

The purpose of this letter, though, is to tell you how to succeed as Jay Leno's replacement.

1. Try being funny.
2. Work on your relationship with Max Weinberg. He's a great drummer, but let him talk instead

RICKLES'
LETTERS
195

of pounding out Indian messages to you on his drums.

3. When you get to LA, have a little class. Don't get up on a ladder to help the workmen take Jay Leno's name down.

There it is, Conan. Great advice. If you don't use it, Ringling Brothers needs a barker.

Your pal,

Don

Mr. Larry King
Los Angeles, California

Dear Larry,

We've been friends for over forty-five years and we've had some great laughs together.

When I watch your show, here's what I see: Trouble with politicians, weather disasters (mostly in Venezuela), mob arguments, movie stars beating up paparazzi—Larry, this is your life, and Ralph Edwards isn't even around to listen to it.

You're the only guy who would ask the president of France, "Don't you think she's too pretty for you?"

Who else would turn to the suspenders manufacturers and say, "My pants are falling down. You gotta make better clips"?

Let's face it: your shirts look like someone threw a bucket of paint on you.

Otherwise, your wardrobe is adorable.

The truth is, Larry, that you're still not ready for a rest home. You're still at the top of your game and don't you forget it. Because I'm not going to remind you.

Love,

A Letter to Me

From a Fan
The Heartland
U.S.A.

Dear Mr. Rickles,

I've been a big fan for a long time. In fact, I've been a
fan since the *C.P.O. Sharkey* days, but the show ended.

After years of trying, I finally got the chance to see
you perform in person at the Running Bear Casino while
recently vacationing in Fargo, North Dakota. What a thrill,
Mr. Rickles. It was the best $22.50 I've ever spent in my
life and you gave me, my whole family, and the rest of the
twelve people in the audience every penny's worth. All I can
say is I hope I'm still going as strong as you at your age.

Actually, I hope I'm doing anything at your age.

But let me get to the point. Thanks for picking on my
weight problem, Mr. Rickles. My family really thought it was

RICKLES'
LETTERS
201

great when you told everybody I looked like the Goodyear blimp. And when you turned to my brother and said, "Hey pal, I'm a friend . . . you're fat," we thought that was hysterical.

By the way, I talked to the black gentleman sitting next to us and he didn't mind at all when you asked how come he wasn't playing basketball.

And we all howled when you asked the German-Japanese couple if they were married. They said yes, and you said, "I guess the family's thrilled."

Anyway, everybody had a good time, Mr. Rickles. We just hope we get a chance to say thank you in person some day.

In a dark alley.

With no one else around.

Your biggest fan,

Larry Dickman
Des Moines, Iowa

DON
RICKLES
202

A Letter to
My Commander in Chief

Barbara Rickles
Beverly Hills, California

Dear Barbara,

I know I'm not easy. But you won me in the lottery, and forty-three years isn't bad.

Sweetheart, I'm not going to embarrass you by describing your beauty, your charm, or your intelligence, but I will say I'm the luckiest man in the world. Okay, so I did chip in to help make you who you are, but that's beside the point.

It's you and me, Barb, and always will be.

Kisses and a big hug.
Your husband,

Don

RICKLES'
LETTERS
205

Letters to My Loved Ones

Dear Larry:

What a warm and loving son you've been to me!

As you know, Lar, in my long career I was never nominated for an Emmy until you came to me with "Mr. Warmth: The Don Rickles Project" that was broadcast on HBO. Then, in a magical moment, it all came together. We were both nominated. The fact that it's a father-and-son project makes it one of the highlights of my life.

You're the best.

Much love,

Dad

RICKLES'
LETTERS
209

The Mann Family
Beverly Hills, California

Dear Mindy, Ed, Ethan, and Harrison,

I'm blessed to have you in my life.

Mindy, you're a wonderful and devoted daughter. You're great with those quick one-liners. I wonder where you got it from? It's been a joy to see you blossom into such a beautiful lady and become such a terrific wife and mother.

Ed, you're a fine son-in-law, and as a bonus you play a hot trumpet.

Ethan and Harrison, you're absolutely perfect grandsons. You're cute, you're smart, you're video champs, and, most importantly, you laugh at Pop Pop's jokes.

Much love,

Pop Pop

RICKLES'
LETTERS
211

Rickles thanks . . .

My terrific children, Mindy and Larry; my grandsons, Ethan and Harrison; and my son-in-law, Ed. If I left anyone out, call me.

Eliot Weisman, best manager in the business. Okay, Eliot, relax; I said it.

Bill Braunstein, longtime business manager who I've never met.

Tony O, for service above the call of duty. Retired from the Italian army to be with me.

Paul Shefrin, my publicist for over twenty years. That's too long.

Joe Mele, world-class musical conductor. Piano lessons wouldn't hurt.

Rob Heller, you're great, but I've decided to end the commissions.

Mel Berger, literary sharpshooter. Someone buy him a gun.

Ritz thanks . . .

Don, King of Comedy.

Geoff Martin, comrade-in-English-prose whose creative skills helped us whip this book into shape.

Forever-loyal publisher, David Rosenthal.

Quick-witted and talented editor, Ruth Fecych. And Michelle Rorke, for the invaluable help.

Agents supreme: David Vigliano and Mike Harriot.

My family: Roberta, Alison, Jessica, Henry, Jim, Charlotte, Alden, James, Elizabeth, Esther, Bob, and all my loving cousins, nieces, and nephews.

My friends: Alan Eisenstock (funniest writer in America), Harry Weinger (finest soul scholar in America), and Tommy LiPuma (baddest producer in America).

And much love and gratitude to Papa Ritz, still going strong at ninety-two.